THE LOVE CODES TRILOGY

BOOK I

Poems to Soothe Your Soul

LAURA KIMMEL

For permission requests, email the publisher at the address below.
E.P. House
hello@ephouse.co

First edition – April 2025
Paperback ISBN: 979-8-3492-5802-2
Hardcover ISBN: 979-8-3492-5803-9

PRINTED IN THE UNITED STATES OF AMERICA ON ACID-FREE PAPER

www.ephouse.co

I dedicate this book to
my glorious son,
may the world shine
as brightly for you,
as you so generously
shine in it.

table of contents

Yet, paradoxically, it is often through encountering its opposites—fear, doubt, hatred—that we become more aware of its presence. The shadows illuminate the light and the discord deepens our understanding of harmony. Rather than resisting the negative, radical love embraces it as part of the greater whole, a catalyst for transformation. In allowing all things to belong, we create space for growth, for healing, for alchemy.

Radical love in everyday life begins in the smallest moments: waking up in the morning realizing we're alive, feeling inhales and exhales, the water we drink, the plants that silently witness and interact with us, the words that we choose to speak and how we speak them. It is a love infused with intention, a love that sees through illusion and understands that many of the thoughts we struggle with are not truly our own. They were given to us by culture, media, and instructions of various kinds. And yet, within that awareness, we hold a quiet power—the power to choose, to rewrite, to return to love.

When we meet another human being, radical love is the knowing that they are already whole. There is nothing to fix, nothing to change, and nothing to make more or less. Just by existing they—and you—are worthy, complete, and filled with the same current of love that flows through us all.

Radical love extends beyond the personal—it reaches into our thoughts, emotions, and bodies, embracing all that we are and all that surrounds us. It is the practice of seeing ourselves and the world with tenderness, of honoring every experience, both light and dark, as part of the vast unfolding of love itself.

And so, with this understanding, my relationship with love deepened further. It was no longer something I simply felt—it was something I witnessed, something I participated in. It became a living presence in my days, speaking to me in ways I had never noticed before. And in this communion with love, poetry began to emerge.

In these moments, I offered what love I could, sharing it through music, teaching, and connection. And during this time, poetry began to emerge more frequently, almost as if it had been waiting for me all along. These poems were not merely words but revelations; lyrics to the music of life. They taught me as I wrote, reshaping my days, my vision of the future, and even my understanding of the past.

Now, I share this love with you—with your heart, your body, your mind, your feelings, your actions, and your wishes. Through these poems that I call Love Codes, I hope to reflect the changes we all experience. Changes born of struggle and pain, changes that herald growth and flourishing, and changes that echo the profound molecular and energetic shifts within us. I offer these words as companions for your journey, words to turn to for comfort, support, hope, inspiration, and above all, love.

Over the years, as I dissolved the boundaries between myself and the living world, I began to perceive love in ways I had never imagined. The lines blurred between me and the plants, between me and the ocean, the sky, and other people. Love revealed itself not as a mere feeling but as a pulsating energy; a force akin to sound that is constantly oscillating, vibrating, alive in everything. Perhaps it spoke to me so vividly because I am a musician, attuned to the rhythms and harmonies of existence.

I began to feel this energy in every leaf, every flower petal, every raindrop. I noticed it shimmering in my fingernails, radiating from the shapes of the moon in all its phases: the full, the half, the crescent, and even the faintest sliver. Love became an electric substance; a current flowing through everyone and everything. But to truly feel it, to see it, often required stillness in myself—a quietness of being—or moments of extraordinary intensity. Sometimes it was exuberant joy that illuminated this love. Other times, it was the profound pain of desolation. In these states of heightened awareness, the love energy became visible, perceptible, and undeniable.

This current of love—this wave, this electricity—is always present. It does not require our search or effort to exist. It is not something to be achieved or earned. Instead, it is a space that we can choose to acknowledge, a space that, once noticed, flows toward us and through us, connecting us to all living things.

This book—and the poems in it—is about radical love. It is my gift to everyone and is an invitation, not a directive. It invites you to step into this space and to let it meet you where you are. As you read these words, know that they are not static. Though they originated from my thoughts, as you take them in, you are recreating them. Your interpretation—intellectual, emotional, and spiritual—breathes new life into them. Each reader expands the meaning, the vibration, and the embodiment of these words, contributing to their growth and resonance.

I am not asking you to become a poet. I am asking you to realize that you *already are one*. Poetry is not confined to verses and rhymes; it is in the way we perceive, the way we feel, the way we connect with the world around us. To live is to create poetry—to shape meaning from the raw materials of existence.

What are the truths this poetry seeks to unveil? They are truths that champion humanity, emotion, and nature. They are truths that champion you, your thoughts, feelings and unique interpretations of these words independent of my intentions and yet co-creating with them. They remind us that vibration—the rhythm of life—touches every cell, every bone, every moment of our being. We are interconnected.

All photography taken by Laura Kimmel

painful journey from transformation

In the midst of each year, each decade, and even in the day to day, I find that movement, change, and transformation are some of the most consistent currents in all of our lives—ironically steady, inescapable, and flowing through us whether we welcome them or not. The moment we feel that we've found "stability," we are suddenly thrown into the wind and quickly find ourselves on flooded ground without a boat. Rarely are these waters, or these winds, calm, both personally and universally. Very often, they wind through high and low terrain of intense emotion, jumps, trips and falls—both positive in nature and painful. Yet within this turbulence, we may discover something profound: inherent resilience. The kind that we don't need to create but is given to us *the moment we're created.*

Sometimes, when things are particularly difficult, each step can become heavy and each breath can become laborious in a sea of deep darkness. Yet, it is in the midst of such struggle, the smallest seeds and farthest stars of light can begin to reveal themselves, finding slight cracks and crevices in which to shine into our hearts.

These poems are humble offerings—gentle lights for the paths you travel. They stand beside you through every stage of transformation, whether you are caught in present upheaval, revisiting echoes of the past, or peering over the precipice of new beginnings. In each verse, may you find a companion for every step, every morning and for every worry—a lantern to illuminate your shifting horizon. May these words offer comfort, and in turn, invite your own voice to rise in gentle echoes of hope.

Through each verse, I wish to remind you that you are not alone navigating. Carrying love, understanding, and quiet strength, I wrote these verses to remind you of your innate resilience whether you can feel it or not. They are to cradle your worries with gentle compassion and to send you sparks of inspiration in moments when you feel you have none. Let their flickers of light remind you that hope and love endure, ever-present beneath the surface, whether you feel them or not ... they are there.

These journeys of discovery and change are both personal and collective. In writing them, I share a view that changes the moment you read it. The joy, pain, and transformation is mine, yours, ours, and the worlds. Though your path is uniquely yours, it is also part of the entire landscape of all existence. As you breathe in this moment, you share the ever-changing air with your surroundings. The air of these surroundings intermingle endlessly and circulate effortlessly with unimaginable speed and covering remarkable lengths of land and space. These poems aim to bridge that distance, offering a space where you feel accompanied, where the shared hum of humanity sings gently in your ear, *where you are not alone.*

With this in mind, these verses are not maps but companions—fluid whispers that support your innate strength of being human and your boundless capacity for change.

These poems are not to deny, ignore, or to diminish pain. These poems are an attempt to both recognize part of the pain that might exist in you, and at the same time are to shine for you in the dark, offering a spark to guide you toward the light of love that resides both within you and on the horizon with the world. May each stanza serve as a quiet promise that you are more connected than you know (even to the other readers reading these poems at different times).

In these times of uncertainty, may these poems help you feel that you can trust that even through the of heaviest storms, there are clear open skies behind them. May they grant you the courage to honor however you feel at any moment. As well, to honor your past, present, and future transformation and lovingly embrace the ever-evolving story that is uniquely, magnificently yours.

Within these changes, transitions, and shifting seasons of life, I offer each poem as a companion, and a reflection of the shared truths binding us all. The miracles of being human and the miracles of the morning and evening each day. They aim not to dictate, but to inspire; not to solve, but to soothe; and above all, to remind you that within every trial of transformation lies a quiet, undeniable brilliance waiting to be revealed.

When we confront transformation through pain, and the possibility of relief within it, we approach a doorway—a portal of sorts. This threshold can feel daunting to say the least, for we feel that we stand fragile, raw, and alone. So many shapes of pain swirl around us—shadows, strikes, and typhoons of circumstance. Whispers and shouts echo through the body: an accident, an injury, a worry. This ache can be relentless, carrying sadness, even paralysis. Along the winding path, questions arise: How do we escape this? What purpose could this serve? Why stay at all?

Even in the depths of what seems solitary, there is always the possibility of change because *pain is never borne alone*. It is a communal thread that binds us to a collective interviewing of human experience.

World pain enters our space and then extends out from our private depths into the world, revealing judgment and conflict. Anger spills from one heart to another, reminding us how deeply we crave a way through.

Yet, despite it's power, while it has it, pain can be a catalyst for something new to appear. Though the entry point, this through-point, seems narrow. However, it can lead to a realm that stretches wide and open, promising more depth and possibility than we dare imagine. And the pain, though unwelcome, can also become an alchemist of sorts, peeling back illusions and stifling restrictions. This exposure brings fresh air of thought and feeling to a renewal, a place where deeper truths may take root and grow in an unimaginable but glorious direction. The smallest flicker emerges, a small but fiery spark illuminating the vast darkness. Like a faint wisp of light, it appears unannounced, offering direction, guidance, and a subtle glimpse of relief. Often invisible in calmer days, it blazes to life when adversity weighs on us the most, and it can because an internal flare that ignites hope. It thrives on self-compassion, on the courage to remain present with pain, to truly know it, and to discover within its depths the endless possibilities of discovery.

When light feels impossible, may these poems find you and offer warmth. Let them shimmer when difficulties seem endless, a beacon to hold when the path is unseeable. Let these poems be a sanctuary; a space to set down your burdens and *simply exist.*

We will venture into the poems together, each verse a light, each word a step, and each page a shared journey through pain, through movement, through change, and into the radiance of transformation. I invite you, all of us, all of you, dear readers. A hand outstretched, a voice whispering, "You are seen. You are heard. Let us walk this path together knowing that lights of all forms, will come to show us the way."

transition

All the love in the world is with you my friend
Though my heart aches for your heart
and I hear the crying in your eyes
You are not alone as the flames rise to the sky

We will sing to you as
Your bones settle and your breath slows

So even with the boulders you carry
You will breathe
You will speak
You will walk upright tomorrow

can i?

Can I expand with the sky I see?
With the ocean ahead
With the water at my feet
Can I let go of all fear?
Let ego just hang out and be
without interfering in front of this vast sea
Can We?

HUMANITY

dry

I cried ten thousand tears
after what I had seen

But they asked me not to
with the water shortage and everything

I thought I might be a good filter
To produce a loving liquid delivery

But I was wrong for with every attempt
I broke the tent
and feared I could never mend it

Will I ever sleep again?

the small sparkle

Do you look for light
in the darkest of times

In the winds of sacred signs
In the petals of closed minds

Do you ever worry that you're also blind
to obvious tides

I do

Then, out comes the sunshine

Three little lights
Of the night sky
Where have you been all my life?

I thought I'd never find them again after the flight

shake

I'm in a terrible state

I've made so many mistakes

There's too much grief to hold

I'm afraid of what I'll create

So I cry with the rain and the wind and the storms that keep everyone awake

Trusting the power and velocity

of this vortex

will move the emotions and world events at stake.

Can we Embrace

the forces of the Earth

to Shake loose the disparities

To disrupt any 'oppressivities'

And to remind all the people who really have

the Seeds

The HUman Beings

the shattered
healing

Sometimes what We think are

Cuts

Broken

Bruises

Of mistakes,

wrecks and finishes snapped

Become the support for our spine

the upright gift of our backs

They end up being the fruited flowers of our hearted souls

not snags

Us, sometimes damaged, injured, hurt and cursed can give us life into the next

chapter

The next verse.

LOVE IS THERE

grief

As grief takes over
I fall to the floor
I sing to sore
Reaching for something more than I'm told
But the truth here and there
is the same from every side

the more we breathe into the vastness of the unknown,
the more we come together,
and the less we hide...

It sure does hurt though sometimes...

together

I'm not allowed
to let my heart
explode in front of you
But if it does I hope it heals us both
and beats in Two...

Is that what pain is for?
to show the snare,
The possibility of repair
the fragility of the wearer

Does it help us remember that
Separateness
Is only a temporary bearer?

hope

A water clear and cool

I hope it clears the air
from what my deepest instincts compelled me to

It was the right thing
but sad and true

A Water Offering

waters receiving

The deepest Love with

Simultaneous solitude

friend or foe?

I am the light and the dark
in the dragon
flying above me

The ancient red and purple messiness of being

Clear crystals sparkle an opening
And I lie here open
and knowing

Love is the only way
to get through the fear
of painful Flowing

the blue sun

Looking for ways to fortify my heart
to
Love without this star for a time

Have you ever lived without the sun in mind?

To remember it's temporary this loss of life
Comes new from inside

As the blue stars penetrate this earth
I remember
that Universal love is at the center of existence
not just at birth

Where do you go
to know
that all is kind
and in kind..
To where it always shines
on the inside

To know
the light of a star burns
forever in a way
as a new one is always born
Because
Our Hearts are more
than we've been told

The Blue Sun

space

I won't allow you to be dead inside
Or to have dead eyes
I will try to help you Feel the juice
raise the game
'There is no shame,' I'll say
I will help you show the sparkle you're made of today

Then I'll remember
that I can't force this way to play
That I can only allow you to say what you want to say
To face what you want to face

and to stand with arms wide

To open the space

Loving

breathing

On the Edge of a cliff
On the edge of a shape shift

Humanity is about to quickly tilt
30 -40 degrees

It insists.

Not many see it coming
and no one can stop those worrying....

For those that sound the alarms lose energy into the void
and the louder they warn the faster everything goes

So I know not to yell & scream...
for the truth of Love is the only way
and it is as gentle and as powerful as it seems

Breathe with me...

a spoken song

I have to sing I have no choice
I have to speak and use my voice
If title waves of rushing sore

Pull me to shore

Please take me in and let me cry
Please take me in and don't ask why
And let me find the pain
the source

Of love's far course

I didn't bring a boat at all
I only have my heart,
It's small

Too small to float alone
In the Ocean's groan
of sweeping melancholy

Save me

within

The ache of the water
The ache of the wind

Where you begin
There is no beginning

There is no swimming or stalling
Just breathing and letting in

empty

The sharks
ate my insides
and didn't leave any left for me

so I was stuck
with saltwater
and seaweed...

Anxiety...

The Love Codes freed me

the healing game

The rawness of the cuts that never came
Have burst open anyway
with the rain.

The constant sewing
could keep me insane

And gosh it stings
when it gets near absolutely anything!

But I'd have much more to gain
if I could accept the tears
that were never there

Allow it to heal itself again...without the strain

fire to ice

Burning flames
Burning turning core

Under feet
Where
From the the darkness of what one could see

Cracking blue
Crackling white
Shines the same

The change is overwhelming
And just the beginning

heart locks

I cry for everything that was
I cry for everything that is
I cry for everything that will be

So, I unlocked my heart
for the 900th time last week

I have only one key left

Please don't take it from me

sapphire star

Letting go
of the yellow sun
So I could follow
the blue star

I had to let my wings burn
And find different fuel
to know where we are

But the shining sapphire
gave me everything I needed
to fly

I didn't need to make anything

was almost too painful until I realized

Home

waterfall

I mend my heart
It breaks again

I mend my heart
it cracks like glass

I mend my heart
and this time

I place it on my head
To lift it from the dread

And let the Love
waterfall down
instead

the power of
vibration

When you see the sun rise—its watercolor vibratory rays of light expanding across the horizon like beams of gold—not only does it illuminate the sky, but it shines on your spirit as well. In those moments, with quiet breath, you can sense the gentle hum of light and of life pulsing around you. It is part of the unspoken promise that love vibrates through all and through you. And when night falls, when night rains, when stars shimmer with giggles and joy, you can feel this same presence—the love bridging dusk to dawn and dawn to dusk. It is in these rhythms, of daybreak and nightfall, of sky and ocean, of sky and self, that we glimpse our connection to a deeper force, reminding us that we are part of something wondrous and that we are made of the same.

These daily miracles are exactly that. The fact that they happen daily can sometimes allow us to forget their power, but they are vibrant indications that our world vibrates with energy—rays of sunshine coloring the morning clouds, stars burning in the darkest nights, each a proclamation of the resonant melody singing through all that lives.

Love itself can be felt within these rhythms, guiding us and encouraging our hearts to open. The vibrations of the Earth—from the subtle shifts in soil to the tectonic movement beneath our feet—can mirror, reflect, and contribute the vibrational patterns of our minds, our connections, and our interactions. We, too, can feel the effect and change shape from the unseen frequencies, by pulses of hope, longing, and deep-seated wonder.

Time, too, moves within these currents, not confined to the strict ticking of a clock but found in the slow sunrise, the tide, and the change from night to day. Dawn arrives with a soft unveiling, offering us a tender moment to awaken to our life's deeper currents. Just as daybreak lifts from night's silence, so do these daily miracles lift our hearts, revealing glimmers of possibility. By embracing this broader concept of time, we free ourselves from the narrow confines scheduled emotion. We can let go of prescribed thought and become travelers through an unfolding and expanding universe light, sound, and feelings. We catch a glimpse of how each moment pulses with infinite potential of time, space, and creation.

The power within these vibrations forms an invisible extension of our humanity. Birds fill the air with energetic music, their singing harmonizes with the sun's rays across the sky like bright ribbons of sound. When we take a moment to listen, we recognize how thoroughly we dwell in an infinite orchestra of existence. From the drums of a distant storm to the gentle rush of our own breath, each vibration signals that life is in constant motion. Our pulse follows this natural cadence, bridging us to the earth beneath our feet and the galaxies beyond our sight. By honoring these shared vibrations, we rediscover what it means to be fully alive.

Nature's symphony and cacophony of sound reaches across the earth's most striking phenomena. The roar of volcanoes, the swirling motion of deep oceans, and the steady crescendo of thunderous clouds all echo the same fundamental truth: *we are part of an ongoing dance of creation.*

These wonders invite us to step outside the boundaries we were given and acknowledge our connection with every living force. Even the quite movement of an iceberg or the subtle shift of a desert resonates with life. In every motion, and in every stillness, nature speaks a language that transcends words. By tuning in, we attune ourselves to the very heartbeat of creation.

These reflections serve as one possible opening to the poems that follow—verses that celebrate the dance of nature, the resonance of our hearts, and the boundless possibilities hidden in every sunrise. I attempt, with you, to capture the intangible, granting shape to mysteries that ask more questions. Shining a light on hope and connectivity, illuminating the unseen that binds us to one another. I shine a light on what we might think and why we think it—how we might feel and why we feel it, and on the lights in you that are beginning to shine. Each poem to be a small spark at any time of your day, igniting a deeper recognition of our shared humanity and new definitions of it.

As you read, you may hear echoes of the same vibrations that bring each dawn and carry us gently into night. You may hear the hidden harmonies that arise when we attune ourselves to the quiet miracles of daily life. The exhalation of breath, for instance, reveals a subtle pulse moving through our bodies, reminding us of the intimate bond we share with the air around us. The engineering of white blood cells, mysterious as it is miraculous, demonstrating the complex universes within each of us—the love encoded deep in our veins. By tuning in to these internal songs, we awaken a heightened sense of wonder a different set of guiding principles, and we can feel the unity of our bodies and spirits in profound harmony with all of humanity.

The poems that follow are not prescriptions but invitations to exploration. I ask that we pause and listen: to the birds announcing the morning, to the thunder rolling beneath our feet and above our heads, to the oceanic surge echoing in our own blood.

These subtle signals can guide us toward a more expansive awareness, one where we acknowledge that the lines separating us from the world are far thinner than we believe. There is no single path to understanding, no definitive roadmap to inner peace, and no one correct interpretation. As you become ready, you create the poems with me. Through your mind, each poem expands and unfolds like a tiny universe, revealing glimpses of unity and timelessness, and uniqueness within you.

As you read, you could think about entering a realm where nature's soundscape, the thoughts of the stars, and human experience converge in verse. Each poem is a reflection of possible questions of life and society, of a pursuit of the truth of the love that sustains us—a quiet yet persistent force that is neither bound by logic nor constrained by time or directives. When you read, you might notice how the heartbeat of creation echoes through metaphors and images, bridging outer phenomenon and inner emotion. I hope you find comfort in these connections, allowing them to mend the perceived rifts between yourself and the broader parts of humanity and Earth's life. In this space it's the vulnerability that helps us discover the intrinsic resilience hidden within every breath.

The poems that follow are invitations to wonder, to listen deeply, and to feel the unseen connections that bind us to the world and to each other. They do not offer singular answers, but open paths to possible discovery, awakening new ways of seeing—illuminating the rhythms of nature, the echoes of time, and the quiet presence of love in all things. As you read, may you find sparks of recognition, moments of stillness, and a deeper sense of belonging. These verses are a reminder that transformation is not a distant horizon; it is already within you, waiting to be felt, heard, and lived.

metronome

Sometimes I sing in the emptiness of time
with a clock hanging over the world
going forwards and backwards

While speeding toward the inevitable truth of expansion,
External interplanetary connection
and fundamental change of the human experience

Don't believe the lies of scarcity
of patentry
or loss of sovereignty

We are the Vibration

searching

A mission, I asked?
A mission for the world?
but Where will I get the moxie
for this Fairytale whirl?
Received the opposites of life
since the combo brings strength,
that's for sure

But do you endure...

An idea
A notion
An artistic potion, a swirling motion,
A path of unknown devotion?

A loving centered knowing
Without the How I struggle to let go of showing

Building in a state of liquid flowing...

Hoping 💛

bioluminescence

When the Light of the Blue comes in
Whether it's the saddest,
the deepest,
or the happiest it's ever been
the Blue
has the Light
of Oneness.
The Light
of the Human Being
inside Us.

BIOLUMINESCENCE

love codes

Who are these supposed code makers
The code takers
The code wreckers
The code spellers
The "code" lifters
The "code" primpers
The "code" plumpers, punchers, thumpers, and manipulators?

They are not
They are impostors

It is not just a few that write the codes my friends
We all do
Not just these few of them

We are the creators...
let's remember

They may say they have the codes, the doors , the roads,
but they lie and fall when the rest of us hold
hands as the rest is shaken

The true codes are flexible, digestible , and unenforceable because
Love needs no coercion, permission, or submission

So a celebration for HUmanithy coming together and going within

WORLDPEACE

song.

soooooooonnnggg.

Sometimes I think,

"What could I possibly say

With the power of the sun

and the movement of the air

When the water remembers every moment

that has begun

and has ever been

Maybe I don't say anything

Maybe I hope we all share it instead

Enjoy it,

Together

And sing "

trust

Gathering the sides
The top
The through
The future
The' bright
The star
How far?
Not too...
Closer than anything that's 'true'
Trying to see it and hear it
Letting go to feel it...

THE LIGHT IN YOU

the cosmic mirror

There's more than a string that connects
There's a limitless effervescence

A canal of unfocus
Unlearning
and joyful intentional ignorance

It's where I like to go
to see
the eternal- internal mirror
Of expansion that can't always be spoken

It's reflected,
Instead,
in a fun-house of sorts

perception

Can I bend the world we're in
Like a prism on a string
Like my heart seems to
inside everything

Or can I bend myself ...
the package I come in
as a water wave in a jar that sings

I'm not sure I can bend all things

Maybe with flight
maybe with wings

Perception
Perspective helps remove the sting

Let's see each other
no matter the name
first
as Miraculous HUman Beings
of this place

bee-ing

With bees flying freely
The honey drips through my pores
As I walk
With a glistening
golden train behind me

Tree beings
hug my soul calling
as this life force
pours out of me

along this Earth journey
Deep through the soil grounding
of rooted belonging
of vibrating Love songs

invisible cycle

Distorted and mirrored
the view of the sane

The ocean sways
and washes away

The endless return of playing tomorrow's yesterday

Why do all the people speak on repeat?

Only Love can crack this game

walk on over...

It's the loop
the loop
the loop
It's breaking out of
the loop the loop the loop

Dharma, karma, string theory, quantum theory, daruma,

By realizing I can just walk on over
to the garden
of more
and more
and more and more...

flowers....

That's what Love is

leverage

The time of things
is the opposite of what I know

And while everything seems extremely slow
I know the engine isn't running on low
(it's a trick)

For the leverage
of deep Love
makes everything flow
Effortlessly

light music

The skies will open

The angels will hear your cries.

But please don't worry

They will send
bright crystalline lights

To accompany you
on your time

winter crystal

Have you ever heard
a snowflake with steel?

It will cut through everything
like lightening

but enter your heart
as the brightest
and strongest
miracle that it is

time travel

When the rainbows are purple,
gold,
and white,
Full of snow

You know Love
is at the center
of wherever you go

and I will go
Where you go
The stream carries me
As time allows it to be

Floating

just in time

Storms swirl near by
but the waves take me on the safest path.

Lightning strikes
but the current gently pulls me
Past

Sharks look hungry but eat larger fish just in time.

We All have this within
But how long can we get by?

By deciding to create a new world in our minds

Together

the future

If creation never ends
and reality
continues to bend

We don't need to worry what message to send
For everything about to happen
has already been

I love unconditionally
So I watch the waves roll in

As I listen to the stars sing
I sometimes fear the storms
I see arriving
Because I know what they can bring

But after the darkness
comes the light within

the sound of time

Writing, composing, creating,
The best!

And also utterly torturous

happiest
loneliest
craziest and deepest bet

Trying to hear the music
that hasn't arrived yet...

Almost Love

which side?

Do you ever have two sides of a day?

Depending on which way you turn?
Things could light up or suddenly burn.

Two opposing ends of Love and hate
swirling as strange mates
I wasn't sure I could escape the mess of sound
Until I realised, my music was going the other way

I just had to turn around

becoming

When the ceiling falls and the walls bend

Do you wonder about all that has ever happened
or been said?

As matter becomes clay and
Emotions become the gateway

To a universe that never ends

voice

I almost didn't speak my heart
It almost darted me alive
In a straight jacket and hard decay

But now that it's open
I can never put it under
and be the same way

I will shine and shout
and sing from Love

as that is the only how
I can be now

and every future day.....

love reveals that emotion is the key

When I wrote these poems they revealed truths I had forgotten, or perhaps never fully understood. One of the deepest among them is how often we struggle to honor our emotions—not because they lack meaning but because we learn to question their validity. From the earliest moments of our lives, we learn to hush our sadness, to temper our joy, to simplify and contain our feelings so they do not spill over and unsettle those around us. "Relax," they say. "Calm down." "There's no need to be sad or to cry." These words, meant to soothe, often serve instead to silence, teaching us that our emotions are disruptions rather than guides. As children, we quickly learn that not only do our tears make adults uneasy, that our sorrow is something to be fixed rather than felt, but that the subtle appearance of discontent itself is cause for concern. Even the gentlest teachers, in their well-meaning attempts to reassure, might murmur, "You're okay, everything's fine," as if our distress were a fleeting mistake rather than a truth in need of space.

And so, we begin to swallow our feelings, to shape them into something more palatable for the world.

In loving homes, among kind-hearted friends, the message persists. "Feel your feelings, but heal quickly. Be as happy as often as you can." Yet, emotions are not inconveniences to be hurried along. They are and begin as the undercurrent of our inner world, calling us to listen, to allow, to embrace each wave for what it is —without urgency, *without shame*.

I have come to understand that when we allow ourselves to fully feel—to open to the rawness, the contradictions, the quiet, the unspoken tides of emotion—we are not surrendering to chaos, but to truth. In honoring the subtleties of our emotions, we honor ourselves, recognizing them not as burdens but as quiet and profound messengers softly whispering wisdom to us that we can easily overlook. It can be challenging to notice them since we are often conditioned to pay attention to only the loudest emotions—the ones that shape our moods and actions, while the softer currents can be missed. These poems seek to validate and to hold space for that struggle and to offer a different way of seeing—one where emotions are not to be silenced, but embraced as sacred wayfinders revealing paths to deeper understanding, nuance, connection, and wholeness.

These verses invite us to recognize what so many of us have been taught to resist —that the very forces we are told to subdue, regulate, or restrain are, in fact, our greatest allies. Emotions are keys, unlocking the doors of longing and fulfillment, of ease and discovery, of creation and release. They are portals into creativity and transformation; moments where we stand on the threshold of something new, where even the most fleeting feeling can become a passageway into deeper knowing. And the beauty of it all is that these doorways do not appear once or twice in a lifetime, but endlessly—in the quiet, in the rush, in the in-between spaces of our everyday lives, waiting for us to step through.

Emotions are not meant to be tamed or feared; they are the pulse of our inner world whispering to us where we have been and where we are meant to go. They are the maps that our hearts hum into existence, guiding us with an unseen, yet undeniable, vibrational force.

The deepest love—the love that sings through the roots of the earth, that lingers in the hush of dawn, and that lights our nights—speaks to us through these emotions. It rises as ecstasy, trembles as sorrow, aches as longing, and steadies as hope, calling us to listen. They are our compass points, tilting us gently when we drift, warning us when we are lost but always leading us. We do not need to suppress, diminish, or regulate them into something smaller or something neater. Instead, if we meet them with quiet attentiveness and if we notice them in their first gentle calls—before they crest, before they seek expression—we open ourselves to a profound choice: the choice to honor them, to move with them, to let them speak without fear, and to learn from them. In this awareness, we do not become overwhelmed but aligned. We remain within the great current of love that flows through all things; the unseen force that connects us, carries us, and, when we surrender to it, brings us closer to ourselves and to one another.

There is nothing broken within us, nothing that must be mended before we are worthy. You and I—all of us—were never meant to be fixed, reshaped, or made into something more "acceptable." We are already whole, already enough, just as we are. But when we soften our gaze, when we open ourselves to the quiet marvels around us—the way light spills through leaves, the quietness of the evening sky, the way kindness lingers in a glance—we begin to remember. We begin to see and feel love, not as something distant but as something we breathe in every moment. And in feeling it, we learn to give it more freely to nurture the love that has always been within us, waiting to be known.

The tree with its broken branches and roots carved with time's imprint stands whole, not in spite of its scars but *because of them*. The flowers—their petals weathered by wind and sun—still bloom with undeniable vibrance. Their beauty is not lessened by imperfection, it is deepened by it. And so it is with you, with me, with *all of us*. Our cracks do not make us incomplete, they are the markings of a life fully lived, of love given and received, of lessons learned in both light and shadow.

Every soul carries wholeness within, even in the aftermath of sorrow, even in the ache of mistakes, even in the moments when we have hurt or been hurt. We are not meant to be polished and unbroken—we are meant to be full and alive in our incompleteness. For it is in our very vulnerabilities that we find our truest strength, our deepest connection to one another.

I write these poems as mirrors, holding up to you the love, the struggles, the quiet triumphs of simply being alive. They are offerings, tender and unspoken, meant to awaken what already resides within you. They do not instruct, they invite. They do not confine, they expand. With every word, I ask you to step into them, to let them dissolve and take new shape in your own heart. These are not just poems to be read, they are to be *felt*. To be written, and rewritten within you, as you embrace the fullness of who you are, who you have been, and who you are becoming.

Close your eyes and feel the way emotion moves within you—an ocean vast and untamed, ceaselessly shifting between stillness and storm. At times, it is a gentle tide, lapping softly at the edges of your awareness, a whisper threading through the quiet moments of your life. Other times, it surges—a tempest rising with uncontainable force, unraveling control, carrying you into the unknown. And yet, both the calm and the chaos are sacred. Both are necessary. For within the swells and silences of this inner sea lies the rhythm of your own becoming.

I invite us all to stop resisting the currents within us, to let the rivers of our emotions flow freely without the heaviness of judgment and without the fear of their depth. Let us allow ourselves to be carried, not away, but toward new terrain; toward places that have been waiting for us. This is the gift of emotion. Even when it feels as though it holds us back, it is, in truth, propelling us forward. It teaches us the art of surrender, the art of creation, the necessity of trust, the beauty of growing into the unknown.

Think of a moment when emotions led *you*.

The quiet bloom of overwhelming gratitude from an unexpected kindness or generosity. The ache of longing that pulled you closer to someone you love. The breathless wonder of witnessing something simple but miraculous. The slow, reverent sadness of a final goodbye. In these moments, you were not merely existing—you were alive. Fully, undeniably alive. And that aliveness is what these poems seek to hold, to honor, to celebrate. For within that depth of feeling lies the essence of what it means to be human: to love, to belong.

For in the end, we are all tributaries of the same great river, weaving through the landscapes of existence, merging, diverging, and flowing toward something vast and infinite. The poems, the emotions, the love—they are ripples of this greater whole, guiding us toward remembrance, toward feeling fully, whether gentle or fierce, whether exultant or aching, no matter where we stand in this moment. Please consider opening your heart to the depths of feeling—to the paradox of constancy and change—and allow these words to dissolve and reshape within you, becoming your own alchemy.

the north star

Looking at the moon I see everything through

The past
The future
The time with you

The solitude
The top of the mountain
The cold iced fountains

The opposite of the heat and what's new

but New, of course, isn't at all
It's just the going upward
and the fall

And then the risky leap surpassing it all

The North Star

the seasons of every moment

The joy
The pain
The winter
The fall

The smile I add
with the sorrow

I feel them all

As the world does

Every
Single
Hour

friends of love

When friends of Love
lift up your heart
You know you'll be okay
from the start
Even with tearful fountains
and weighted mountains
Of leaded emotions
and moving notions
With friends of love
you know
that light is on the way
in the sky
and at your feet

And so my friends,
I feel, I cry,
and with the deepest gratitude,
I dare to speak

Thank you

liquid gold

Six hours ago and two hours tomorrow
I was twining taffy
tethered to the melting floor
Often, though, I'm fire
nothing more than air lit
from a gasoline memory of fading speed
So I Call on the water for me
Chrysalis Chrystalline
and put me under the waterfall of ...
Not serene
but the liquid ignition that comes with the feeling

high tide

The Love in my heart blew
in from the ocean
and arrived behind my eyes

to wash away fear and pride

I smiled to hide

and held my heart to try

I hope I can find my ocean on the inside

Only Love could have brought you by
I will remember that when the tide is just too high

the light of lumination

In one night
and in one hundred billion years
at the same time

I felt the coal formation
of the earth's inner crust

But in my mind

My mind's crustation
though it was not frightening
but strange and familiar
rigid and flowing
Hot and freezing without any knowing

And then all of a sudden

A bubbling aeration
A frothing sensation

A white brightness of the situation
broke through
and made room

for the Light of Lumination

Love

sky tears

I thought the sky was crying

but it was the bright eye
of the moon shining

the Moon

Shining the Emotion
of the whole world
through

each other

The sky in the water
The water in the sky
The curious cotton love pillows billow

I watch them comfort
I watch them cradle
I see them fly and sing and cry

And I'm devastated every time they leave to say goodbye

a new day

Sometimes the Fear
of commitment
of failure
of no savior
burns colder than ice

But the sun comes up every morning...
And my heart melts again

whooshed

The past flew in as a dragon force
Dragon teeth
Dragon head
Then a kind dragon fly

I didn't know I needed to cry...
But the flames moved down and around
With a whooshing sound

I hadn't died...

The reds turned
became wisps of blue and purple mist
as I enjoy being alive

dreams awake

I never dreamed of ...
One.
I never had the chance
I was always running too fast
I'd get knocked and
shoved and bent
I'd get back up again and again

But then you
appeared and all was
heaven sent

I decided I'd walk slowly and risk losing everything "spent"

to find out what Love
from this Earth is like

How Love is really meant...

learning

The tears of the skies are in my eyes
Along with the clear blue of it
to the left,
to the side

So glad I can see it or I'd cry all the time

And I do cry

with both true Love
and deep pain
Inside

Learning

light pillar

So the tears fall
and the weight drops away

because now...
the Future,
the Past
and the Bright
Blue Light

are always
One
with my
Heart

Every
single
Day

pressure

I held the door to my heart
as long as I could

But the pressure was so great
I could not contain
the purple, the red, the amber
the flames

For Loving,
I'm grateful to say,
is the only thing I can do these days

day and night

He brought her to the moon
She kissed his hands and feet

They intertwined and intermind
For nothing was as kind as these

As floating

to the gleaming beam
of the galaxy
where they meet

Only at Midnight

the wave

Creating with Love
sometimes feels

hysterical
a miracle

groundless
boundless

like flying
but without wings
without balance

falling
soaring
sighing
diving
a mess.

trying desperately to catch a wind to float on
and rest.

seeing

The Overwhelming
Multiple sides, tides, and minds

I'm lucky I can see a few of them sometimes

But now,

The tears of the skies
are in my eyes
Along with the clear blue

To the left
To the side

Thank God I can see it
Or I'd cry all the time

And I do cry

with both true Love
and deep pain inside

epilogue

Thank you all for reading and for going on this journey with me. While this is the end of this first book, it is truly the beginning of a larger experience—a trilogy that, if you choose, we will explore together. This marks the gentle beginning of a shift in perspective, softly reminding you that this moment is merely a threshold—an open doorway inviting you, inviting us all toward deeper exploration. It is the beginning of quiet, of passion, of resting and knowing, and of the most loving acceptance. This book is a start—a tender spark of the light you have created and are continuously creating, simply by being alive. It is a beginning that draws not from the pages themselves, but from the generous contributions of your thoughts, your time, and your heart. As you read and process, it transforms. It becomes something entirely new with you and with those reading with you. While these poems began with my perspective, they have evolved into being something new as you read them.

Because, you see, this book—these poems—are really about you. *You*, the person holding these words in this very moment. It is about *your* life, *your* feelings, *your* pain, *your* joy, and the vastness that is you.

It is not a set of instructions, nor a guide, nor a doctrine. It is simply a window cracked open to let in a little fresh air—to awaken something, perhaps, that has been longing to breathe.

It is the release of control; the loosening of the grip of others' thoughts and judgments. It is the embrace of our own bodies, our own intricate mechanics, and the symphony of thoughts and feelings within us. What would it mean to let go? To open our hands, to open our hearts, and to allow love to move freely through us, as it was always meant to?

Radical love—that is what these poems are truly about. Not the fleeting kind, nor the conditional kind, but a love so profound, so boundless, that it shakes the very foundations of who we believe we are. A love that does not demand to be returned, does not ask for perfection, does not shrink in the face of fear. This is a love that embraces all things, everywhere, in their rawest and truest forms.

This love begins with *you*.

You are the reflection—the glistening surface that holds the image of the world around you. You are the water—ever-flowing, ever-changing, carving pathways through the toughest stone and the strongest metal. You are the light—the brilliance that illuminates even the darkest bends, that turns shadows into stories, that guides the way.

Radical love is not a destination; it is a practice, a way of being. It asks us to soften, to surrender, to trust. It calls us to examine where our thoughts and feelings come from, to hold them gently in our hands, and then to open and expand further into the life we wish to create. It invites us to wonder: Who am I when I love without condition? What happens when I extend that love not just to others, but to myself; to the parts of me I have been taught to hide? What happens when I extend that love to the thoughts, feelings, and parts of me, that I may not always like?

Perhaps this is what we are all searching for—a radical love in all things, everywhere. A love that whispers to us in the quiet moments, in the spaces between words, in the stillness of our breath. A love that reminds us that we are not alone, that we are part of something vast and sacred and eternal.

This is the first transition of three books of poem; poems that I hope soothe and accompany your sparkling soul. And like all beginnings, it is tender and uncertain. It asks for your patience, your curiosity, your willingness to step into the unknown. It asks you to trust that you are already whole, even as you continue to grow and change. It asks you to believe that love—radical, unrelenting love—is your birthright.

As you journey through these pages, know that you are not just a reader; you are a co-creator with me. Your thoughts, your feelings, your very presence bring this work to life. It is no longer mine; it is *ours*. Together, we are weaving something new, something alive, something that cannot be contained within the boundaries of a book.

You are the reflection. In the stillness of your being, the world sees itself anew. You hold the power to transform what you touch, to bring understanding to chaos, to find beauty in what others might overlook. Your reflection is not static; it dances with fairies in the trees and mist and with the sparkles on the water— ever-changing, ever-becoming.

Radical love begins with a relaxed choice. It begins with the decision to look at yourself with the same tenderness you might offer a dear friend. To hold your own pain with compassion, to honor your joy without reservation, to celebrate your existence as a miracle in itself. It does not always feel easy to move in this direction, but the road becomes extraordinarily clear and kind as soon as you begin.

This love ... this radical love ... does not end with you.

It extends outward, touching the lives of those around you, rippling through your community; your world. It reminds us that we are all connected, that the boundaries we perceive are but illusions. It calls us to relax as we act, to relax as we create, and to relax as we give—not out of obligation, but out of the overflowing abundance of our hearts.

And so, these poems are not just about reading; they are about *becoming*. They are an invitation to continue with the next two books, to step into the fullness of your being, to embrace the sacredness of your existence, to live in a way that explores the radical love that is your essence. It is a call to remember who you are —not just a reflection of water or light, but all of these things and more.

You are the beginning. You are the knowing, the realizing, the accepting. You are the light that creates and is created, the love that moves through all things. And this, dear reader, is your moment. This is the start of a story that you write, a love that you receive, glide through, and give.

And a life that only you live.

Let this be the moment you release control, moving boldly and openly into the mystery of the unknown. Let this be the moment you say yes—to love, to life, to *yourself*. For you belong here, rooted deeply in the shared miraculous heartbeat of humanity and the creation power of radical love.

This moment is not an ending, but your radiant, powerful beginning.

about the author

Laura Kimmel is a poet, composer, singer, and multimedia artist whose creations illuminate the unifying power of sound, language, and imagination. Her debut poetry collection, "THE LOVE CODES TRILOGY: Book 1," serves as a crucial expression of this unifying endeavor, bringing together poetic insight with artistic innovation.

As a global performer, Laura has performed for diverse audiences across Brazil, Italy, London, Japan, and the United States. Notably, she has performed with the Tokyo Symphony Orchestra and recorded for Japan's national broadcaster, NTT, demonstrating her versatility across cultures and mediums. Her extensive artistic repertoire seamlessly blends opera, theater, recital, and television, delivering performances rich in emotional depth and profound musicality. Originally trained as a classical singer, Laura now infuses her vocal and compositional styles with jazz influences and genre-bending experimentation, continually expanding her creative horizons.

In addition to her solo work, Laura collaborates and composes with Blue Écos, an international ensemble dedicated to boundary-defying music that merges diverse styles and voices into a vibrant, shared musical language.

Deeply passionate about the transformative power of art, Laura champions sound, language, and creativity as vital forces for inspiring connection, healing, and unity across borders and hearts. She advocates nurturing essential human qualities such as emotional intelligence, creativity, and physical awareness, ensuring humanity remains central to artistic expression, even as society navigates the growing integration and partnership with artificial intelligence.

www.ingramcontent.com/pod-product-compliance
Lightning Source LLC
Chambersburg PA
CBHW070245300425
25945CB00012B/983